Disney CLASSICS

Disney characters and artwork © Disney Enterprises, Inc.

ISBN 978-1-4234-4179-3

WALT DISNEY MUSIC COMPANY
WONDERLAND MUSIC COMPANY, INC.

DISTRIBUTED BY

HAL•LEONARD® CORPORATION
7777 W. BLUEMOUND RD. P.O. BOX 13819 MILWAUKEE, WI 53213

Visit Hal Leonard Online at
www.halleonard.com

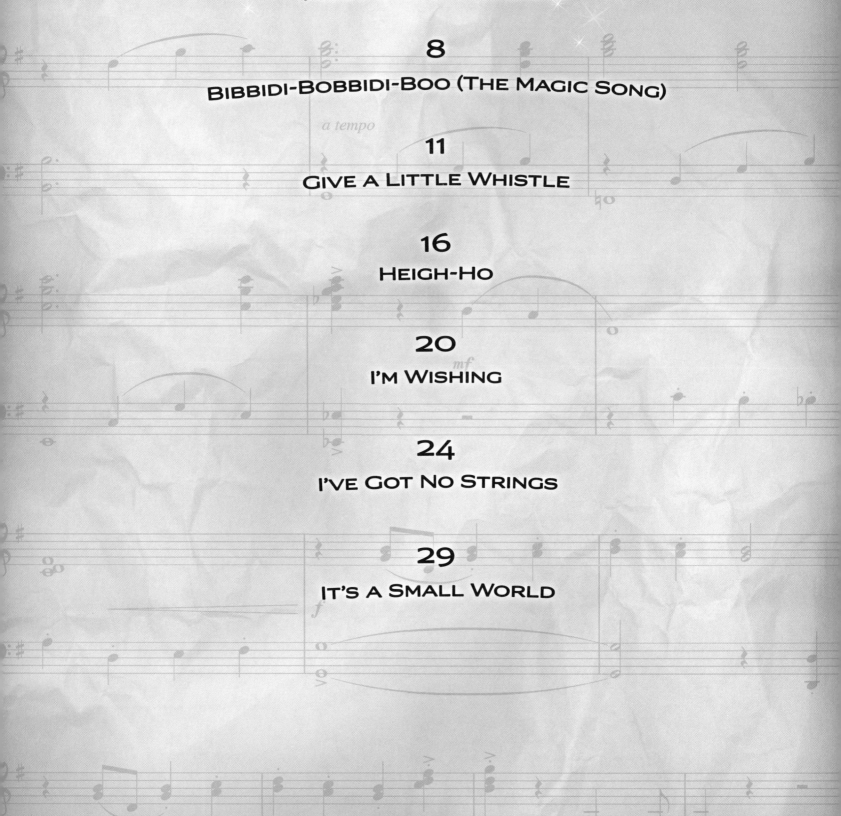

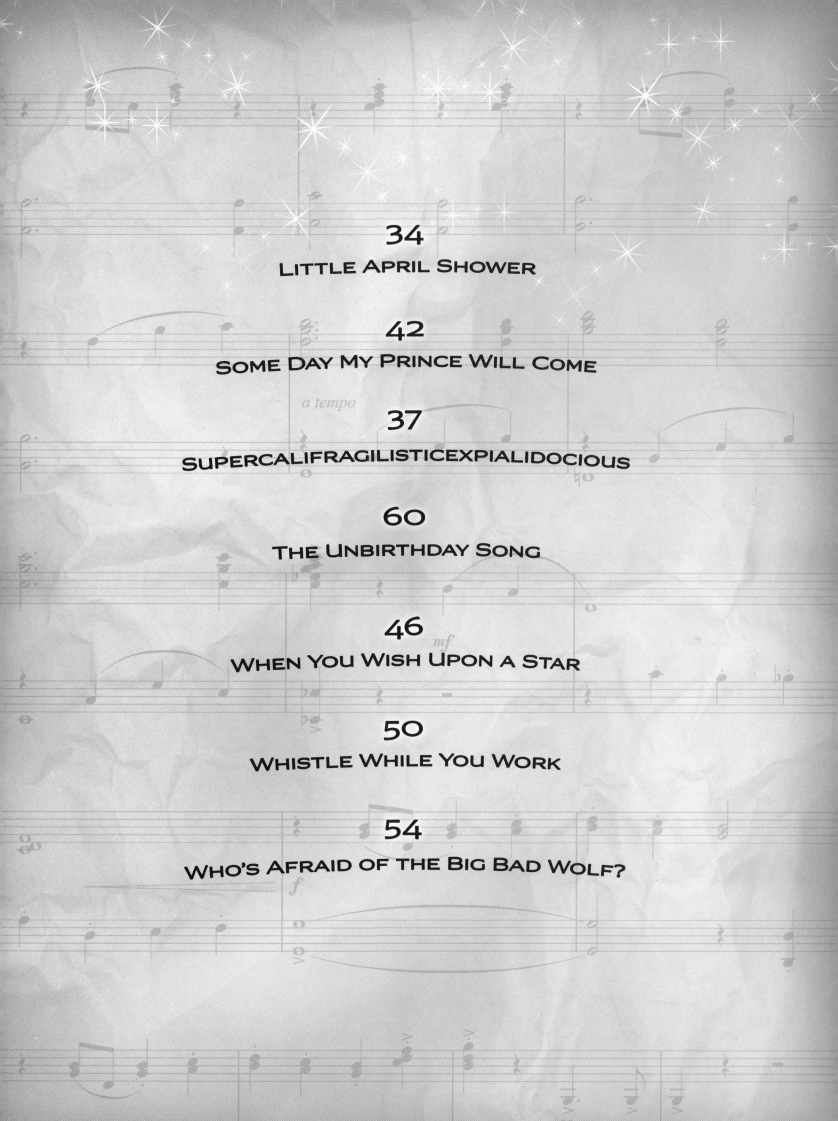

ALICE IN WONDERLAND
from Walt Disney's ALICE IN WONDERLAND

Words by BOB HILLIARD
Music by SAMMY FAIN

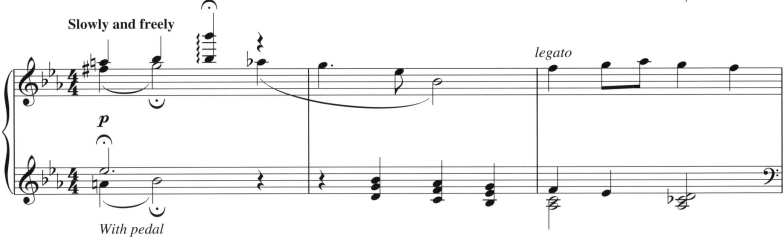

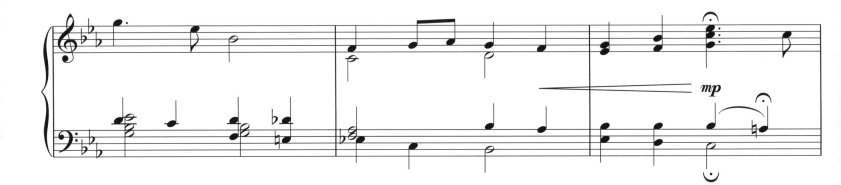

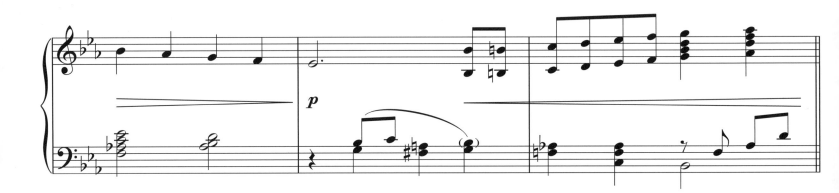

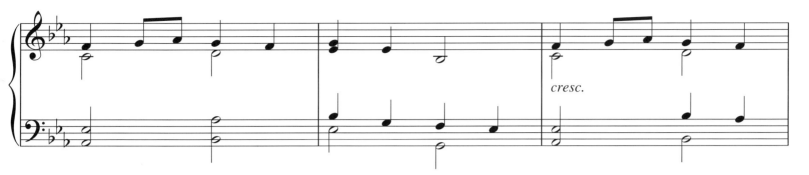

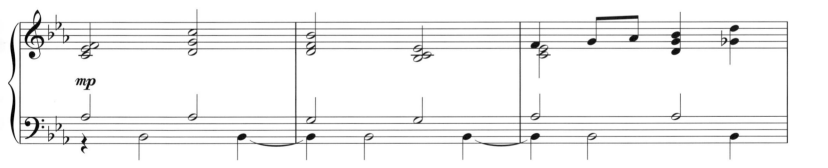

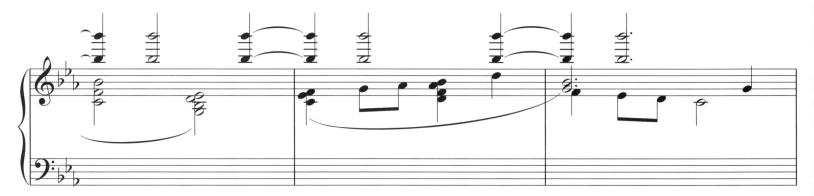

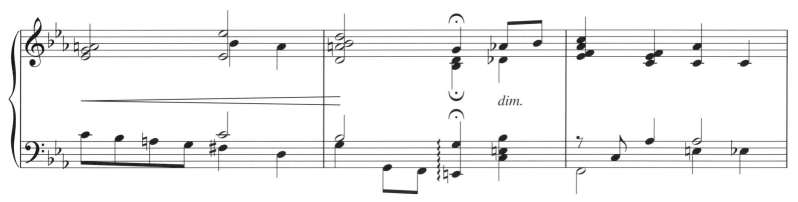

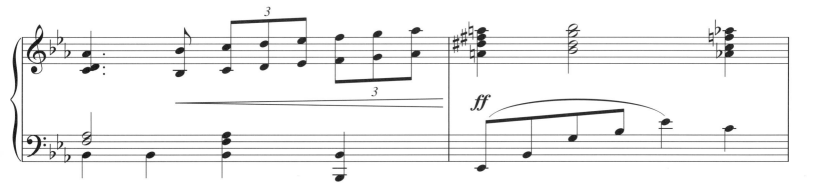

BIBBIDI-BOBBIDI-BOO
(The Magic Song)
from Walt Disney's CINDERELLA

Words by JERRY LIVINGSTON
Music by MACK DAVID and AL HOFFMAN

Bright March tempo

© 1948 Walt Disney Music Company
Copyright Renewed
This arrangement © 2008 Walt Disney Music Company
All Rights Reserved   Used by Permission

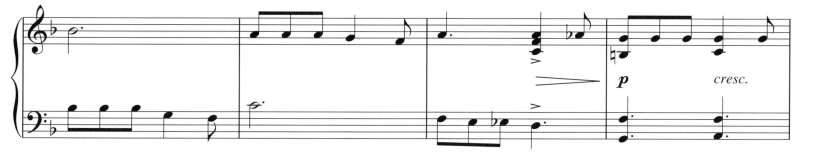

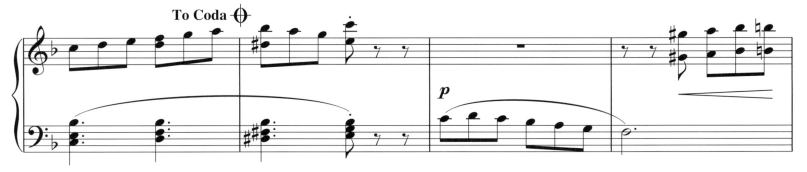

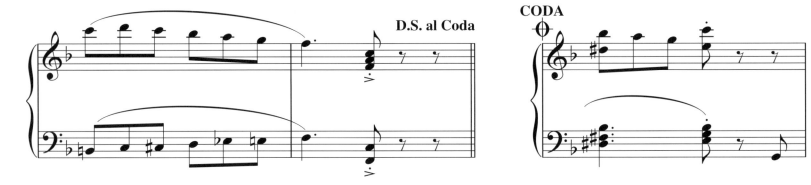

GIVE A LITTLE WHISTLE

from Walt Disney's PINOCCHIO

Words by NED WASHINGTON
Music by LEIGH HARLINE

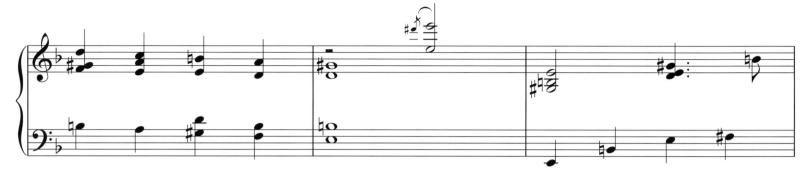

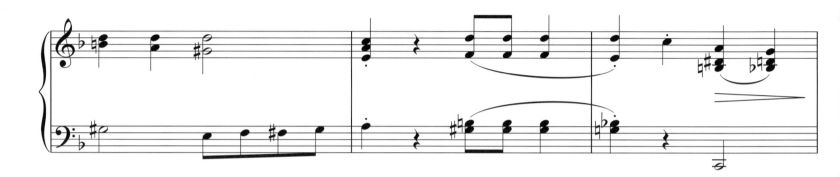

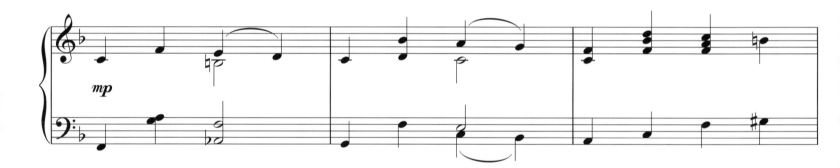

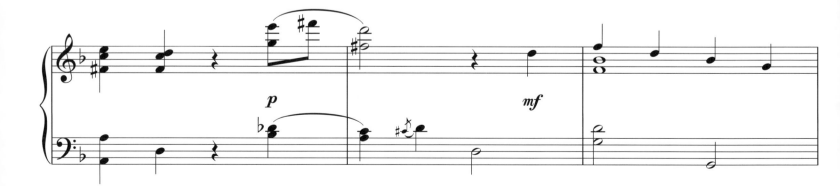

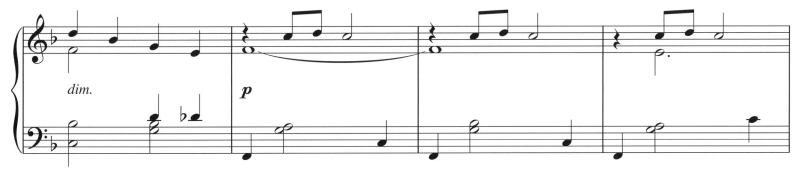

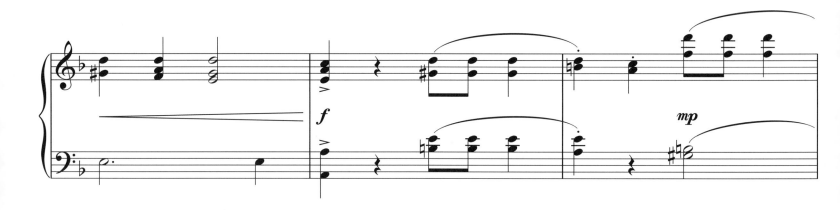

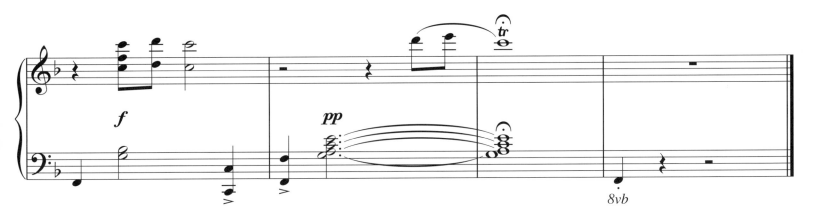

HEIGH-HO
The Dwarfs' Marching Song
from Walt Disney's SNOW WHITE AND THE SEVEN DWARFS

Words by LARRY MOREY
Music by FRANK CHURCHILL

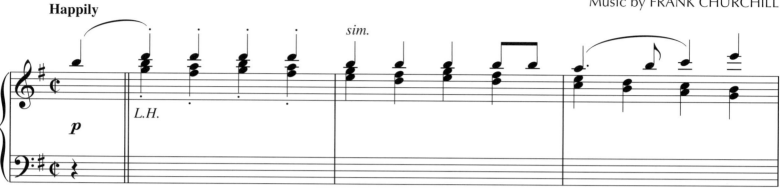

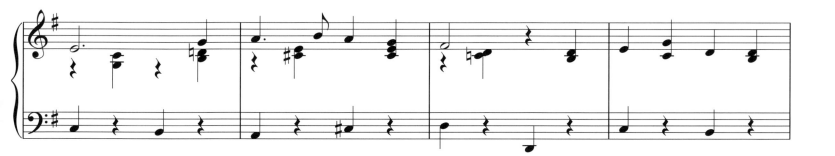

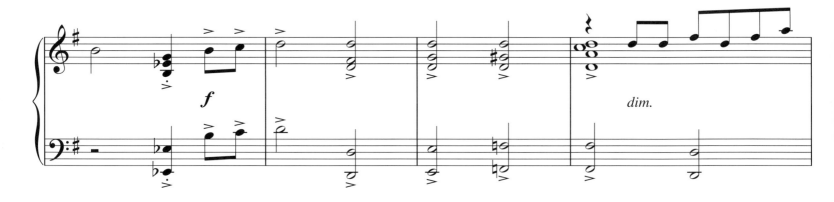

D.S. al Coda

CODA

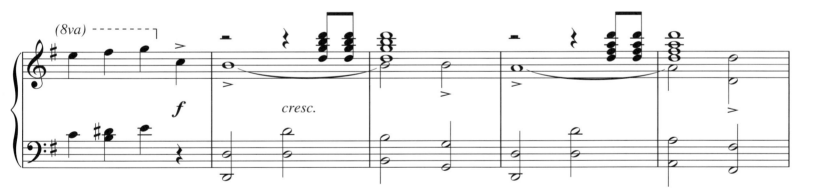

I'M WISHING
from Walt Disney's SNOW WHITE AND THE SEVEN DWARFS

Words by LARRY MOREY
Music by FRANK CHURCHILL

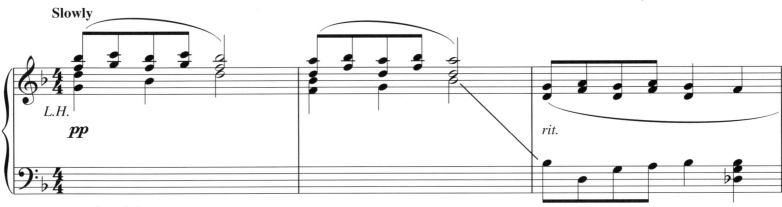

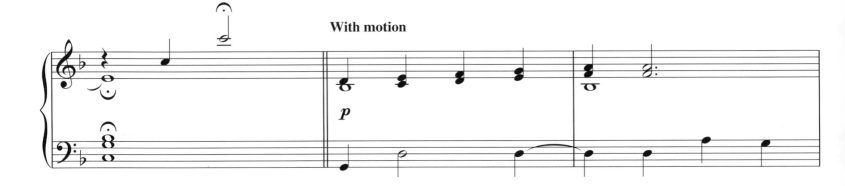

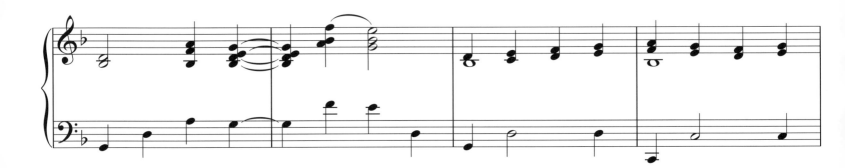

Moderately

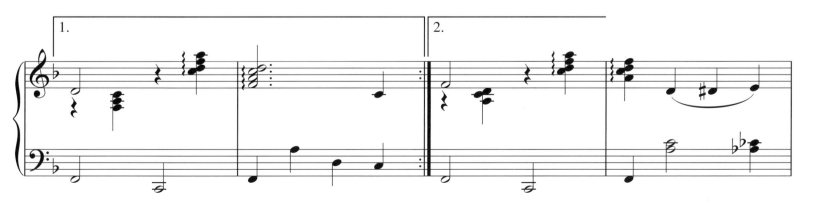

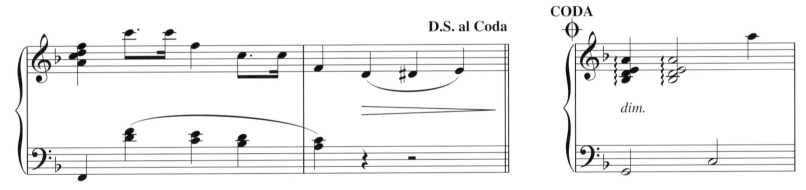

D.S. al Coda

CODA

dim.

p

dim.

pp

I'VE GOT NO STRINGS

from Walt Disney's PINOCCHIO

Words by NED WASHINGTON
Music by LEIGH HARLINE

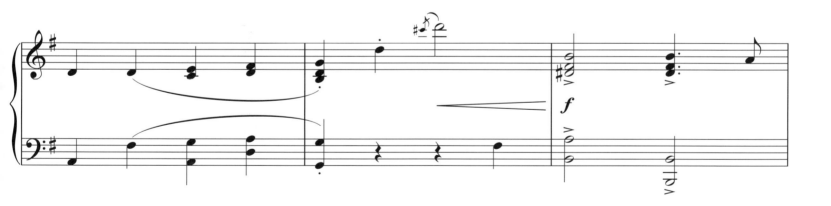

28

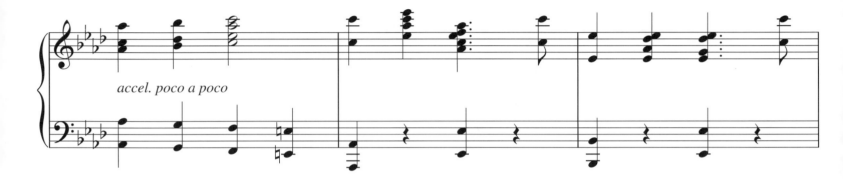

IT'S A SMALL WORLD

from "it's a small world" at Disneyland Park and Magic Kingdom Park

Words and Music by ROBERT M. SHERMAN
and ROBERT B. SHERMAN

Brightly

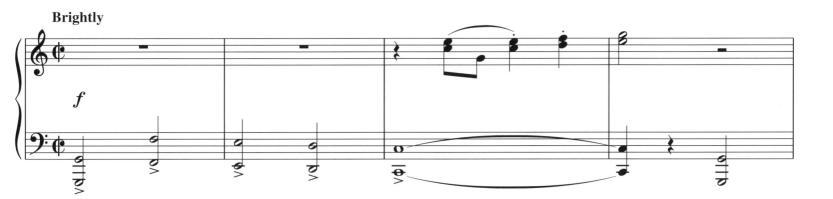

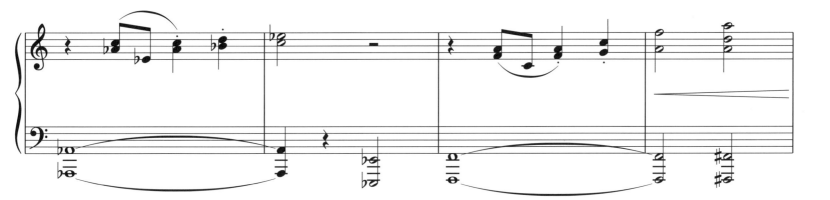

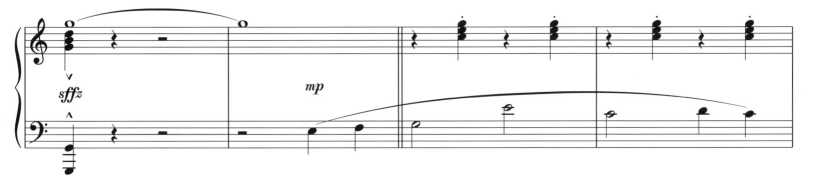

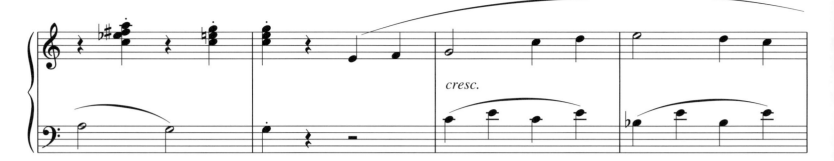

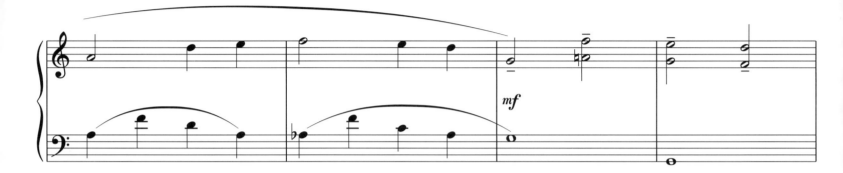

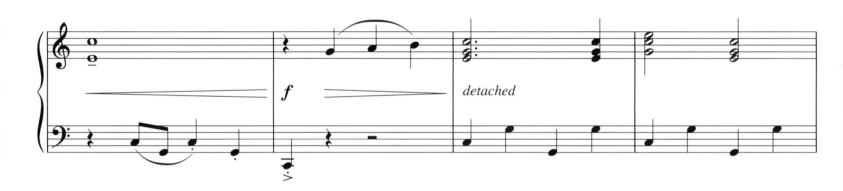

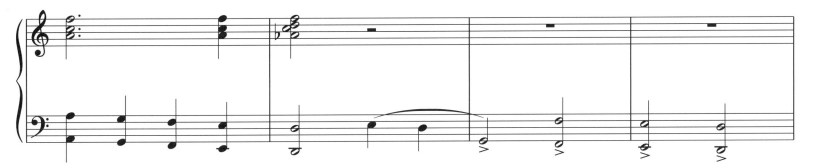

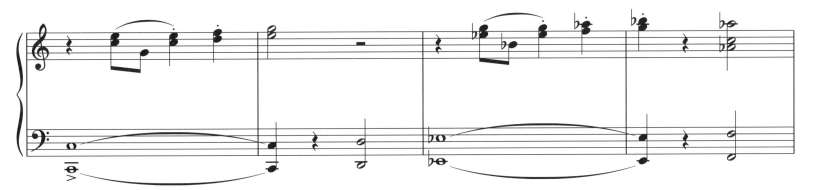

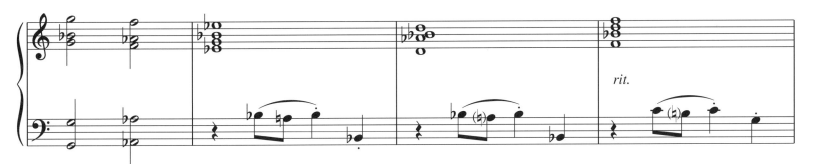

Playful Waltz

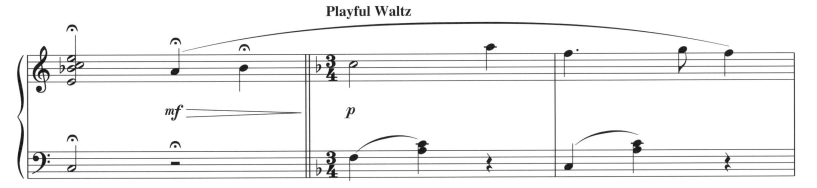

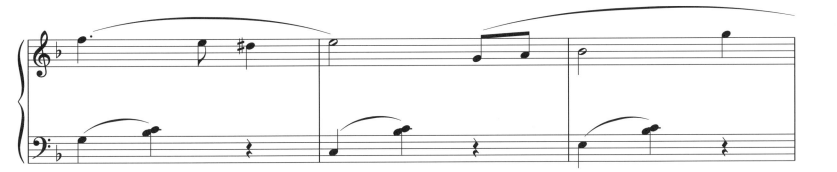

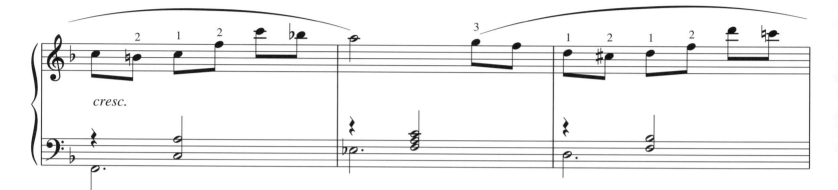

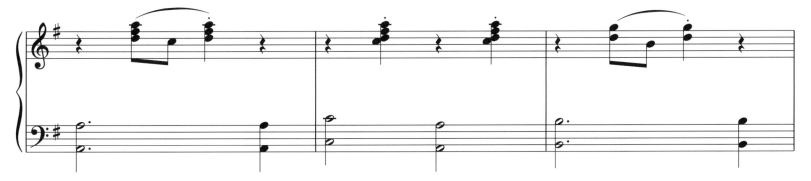

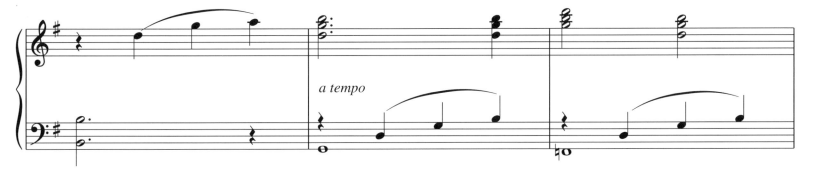

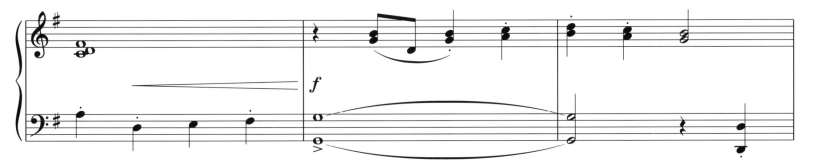

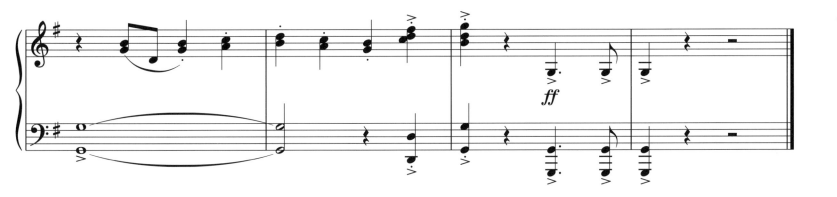

LITTLE APRIL SHOWER
from Walt Disney's BAMBI

Words by LARRY MOREY
Music by FRANK CHURCHILL

Moderately

With pedal

(No pedal)

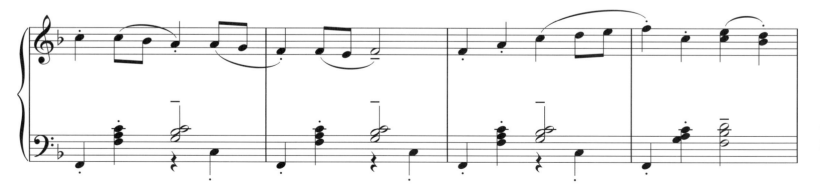

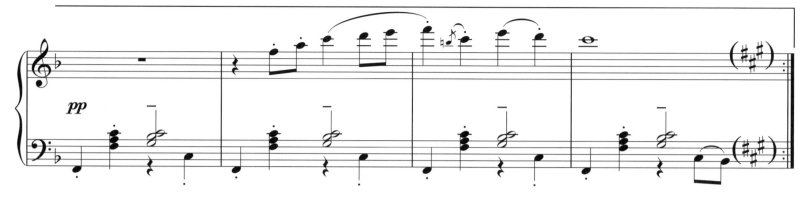

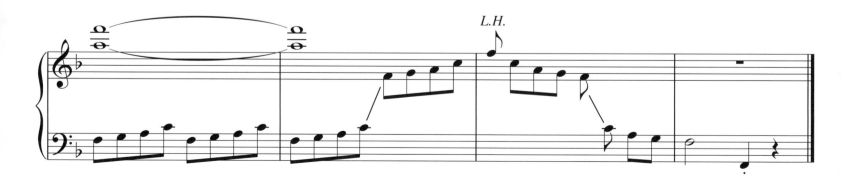

SUPERCALIFRAGILISTICEXPIALIDOCIOUS

from Walt Disney's MARY POPPINS

Words and Music by RICHARD M. SHERMAN
and ROBERT B. SHERMAN

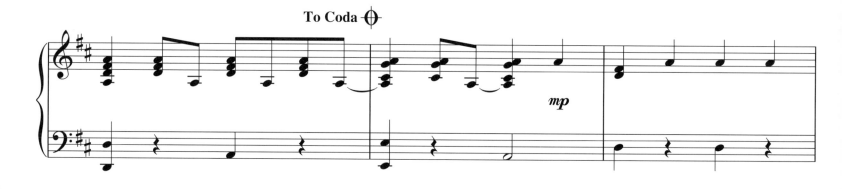

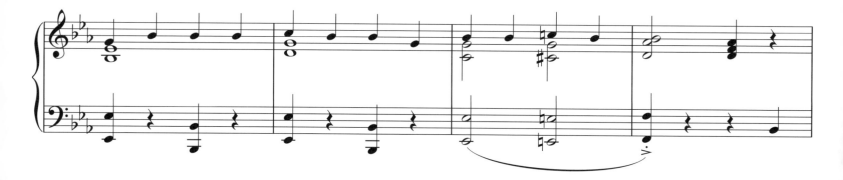

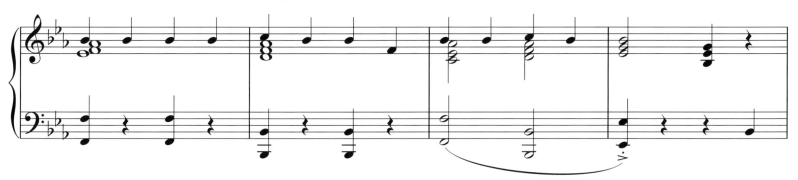

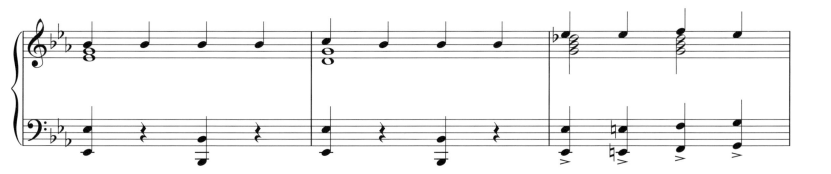

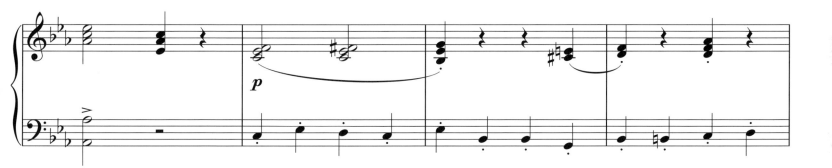

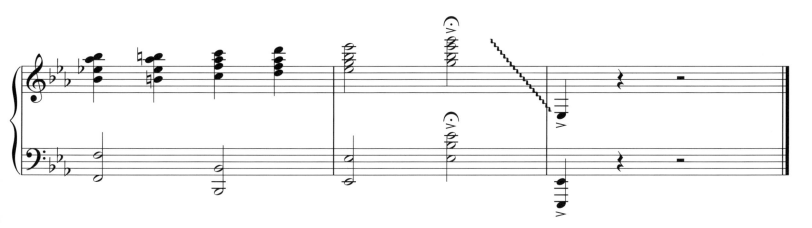

SOME DAY MY PRINCE WILL COME

from Walt Disney's SNOW WHITE AND THE SEVEN DWARFS

Words by LARRY MOREY
Music by FRANK CHURCHILL

Slowly and freely

Moderate Waltz

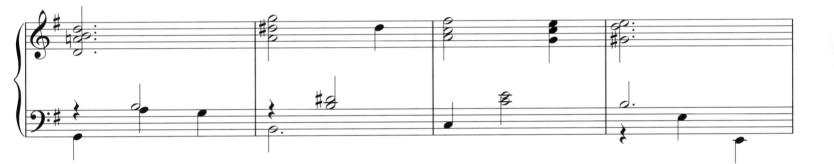

WHEN YOU WISH UPON A STAR

from Walt Disney's PINOCCHIO
featured in THE WONDERFUL WORLD OF DISNEY

Words by NED WASHINGTON
Music by LEIGH HARLINE

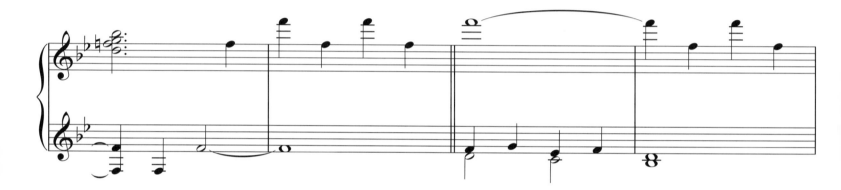

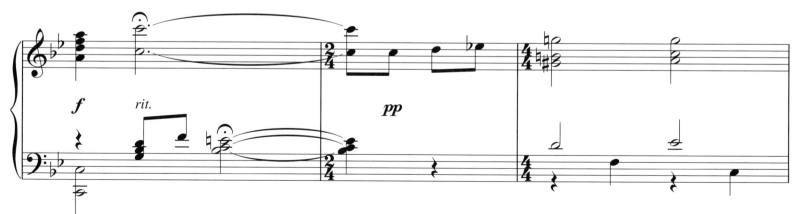

Moderately, with freedom

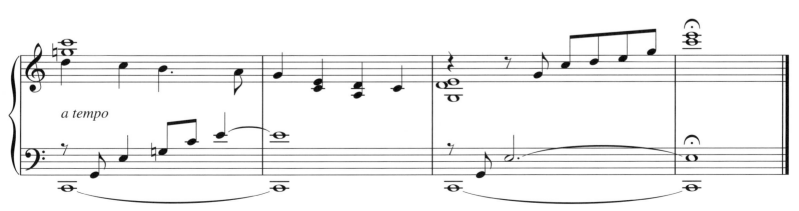

WHISTLE WHILE YOU WORK

from Walt Disney's SNOW WHITE AND THE SEVEN DWARFS

Words by LARRY MOREY
Music by FRANK CHURCHILL

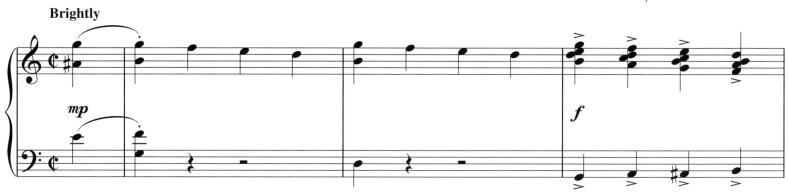

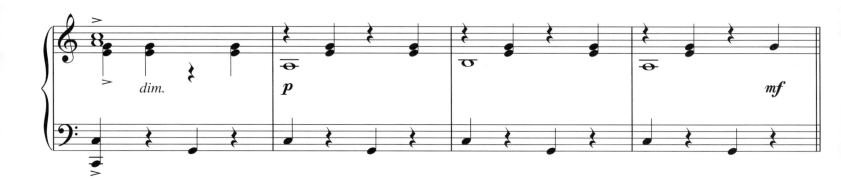

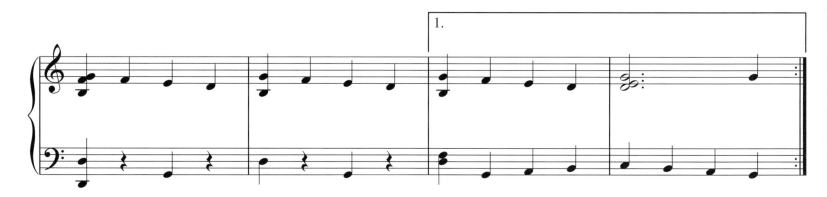

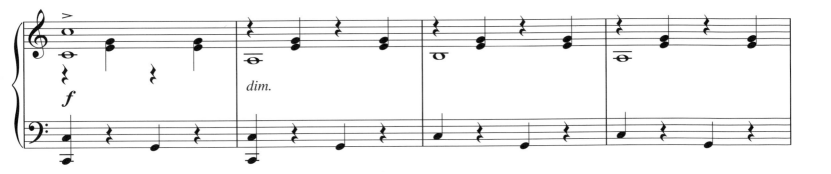

WHO'S AFRAID OF THE BIG BAD WOLF?

from Walt Disney's THREE LITTLE PIGS

Words and Music by FRANK CHURCHILL
Additional Lyric by ANN RONELL

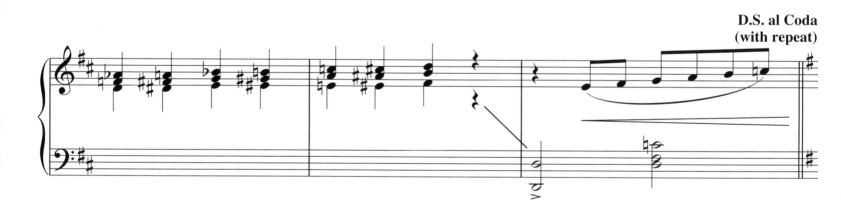

D.S. al Coda
(with repeat)

CODA

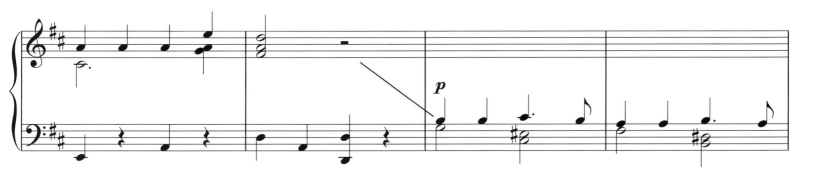

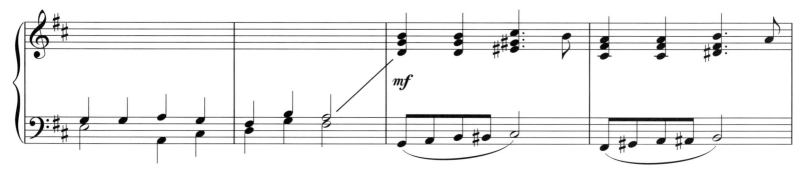

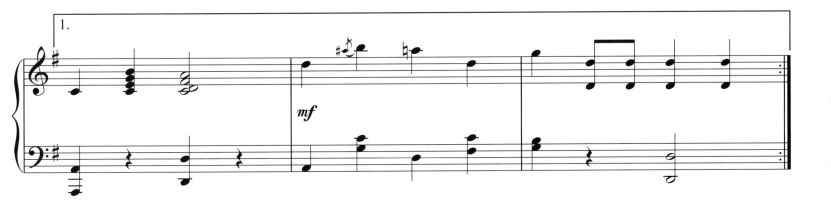

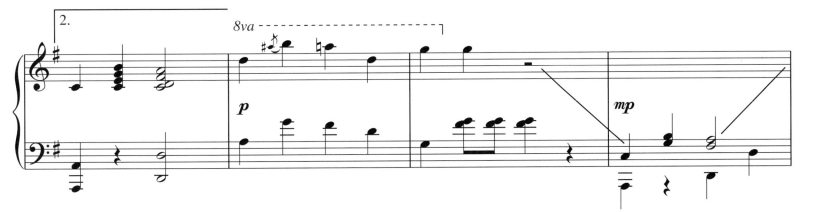

THE UNBIRTHDAY SONG

from Walt Disney's ALICE IN WONDERLAND

Words and Music by MACK DAVID,
AL HOFFMAN and JERRY LIVINGSTON

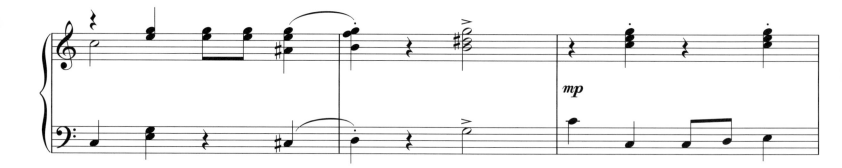

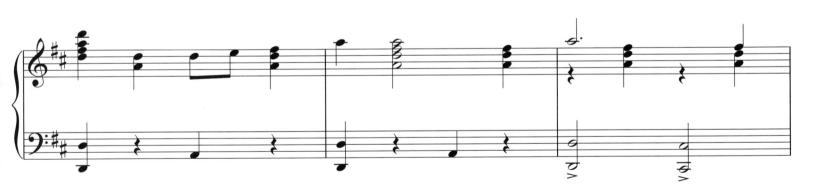

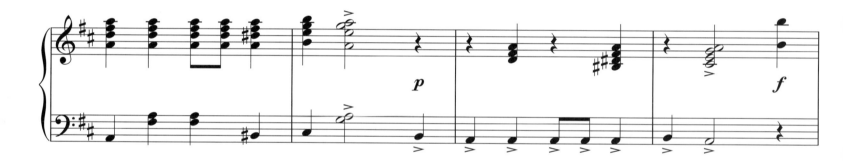

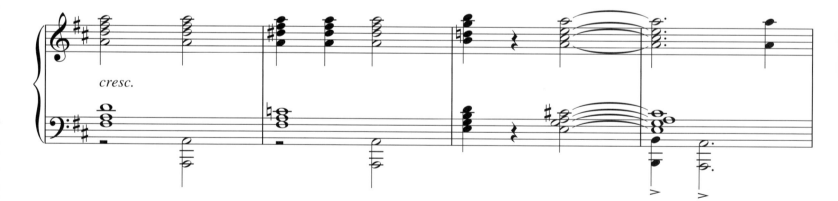